NEWTOWN

Terry Allsop was born in London in 1940 but moved to
Grimsby in 1944 because of bomb damage to the family
home. Moving back to the Thames Valley in the 1960s,
Terry worked for several architectural practices and it
was whilst he was employed at the Reading office of
Broadway & Malyan that he was charged with recording
each building in every street of a 16 acre site about to be
demolished and redeveloped. The author re-discovered
the negatives for this collection of photographs on his
retirement and staged two exhibitions in conjunction with
Reading Library in 2009 and 2011.

Also published by Two Rivers Press

Believing in Reading: Our places of worship by Adam Sowan
Broad Street Chapel & the origins of dissent in Reading 2ed. by Geoff Sawers
Bikes, Balls & Biscuitmen: Our sporting life by Tim Crooks & Reading Museum
The Reading Quiz Book by Adam Sowan
Bizarre Berkshire by Duncan Mackay
Birds, Blocks & Stamps by Robert Gillmor
Reading Poetry: An Anthology edited by Peter Robinson
Reading: A Horse-Racing Town by Nigel Sutcliffe
Eat Wild by Duncan Mackay
Abattoirs Road to Zinzan Street: Reading's streets and their names by Adam Sowan
Down by the River: the Thames and Kennet in Reading by Gillian Clark
From the Abbey to the Office: A Short Introduction to Reading and its Writers by Dennis Butts
A Much-maligned Town: Opinions of Reading 1126–2008 by Adam Sowan
A Ladder for Mr Oscar Wilde by Geoff Sawers
A Mark of Affection: The Soane Obelisk in Reading by Adam Sowan
Roots and Branches: The Centenary History of Battle & Caversham Libraries by David Cliffe
The Stranger in Reading by John Man, edited by Adam Sowan
The Holy Brook by Adam Sowan
The Monmouth Rebellion and the Bloody Assizes by Geoff Sawers
A Thames Bestiary by Peter Hay and Geoff Sawers
Sumer is Icumen in by Phillipa Hardman & Barbara Morris
Charms against Jackals: 10 years of Two Rivers Press edited by Adam Stout and Geoff Sawers
The Ancient Boundary of Reading (map) by Geoff Sawers and Adam Stout

NEWTOWN

A Photographic Journey in Reading 1974

Terry Allsop

TWO RIVERS PRESS

First published in the UK in 2012 by Two Rivers Press
7 Denmark Road, Reading RG1 5PA
www.tworiverspress.com

ISBN 978-1-901677-88-1

2 3 4 5 6 7 8 9

Two Rivers Press is represented in the UK by Inpress Ltd and distributed by Central Books.

Cover & text design by Kirstie Smith and Zoe Rockson and typeset in Pragma and Avenir.

Printed and bound in Great Britain by Ashford Colour Press, Gosport.

I dedicate this book to my brother, John, who lost his fight against cancer on 11 November 2003. It was John who gave me the Exacta VX 1000 camera with which I took the photographs in 1974. I hope it is a fitting tribute.

Sadly, it must also be dedicated to Brenda, our friend for almost 40 years. She lost her fight for life against the same dreadful disease. She was taken from us on 11 May 2012. She was a very special person and will be sorely missed.

ACKNOWLEDGEMENTS

First, of course, I must recognise the help, support and most of all the patience of my wife, Nicola. We met as we both worked for Broadway & Malyan, the architects responsible for the redevelopment of Newtown and we continued to work together there until I retired in 2005.

Secondly, I must acknowledge the person who has really made this book become a reality. That man is David Cliffe who has contributed so much to bring about its publication. David, in his Foreword, refers to the meeting we had at Reading Central Library in 2008. The resulting exhibitions in 2009 and 2011 have been fully recorded in the Foreword and in my Introduction. I must however finish by saying once more, thank you David.

I have, of course, contacted Broadway Malyan (the 'and' was removed from their trading name in 1988) to let them know the name of the practice appears on more than one occasion. As with acorns and oaks, I have been asked to point out that Broadway Malyan have grown into a Global Architecture, Urbanism and Design Practice. This I am happy to do.

I would also like to put on record all the hard work, help and assistance shown and given to me by Kirstie Smith and Zoe Rockson at The University of Reading, Department of Typography and Graphic Communication.

FOREWORD

It gives me great pleasure to write a foreword to this splendid collection of photographs.

When in 2008 Terry Allsop approached me at Reading Central Library, where I was working as Local Studies Manager, to say that he had the negatives of some photographs of the Newtown area of Reading, I was interested. When I scanned the negatives and saw the pictures, I was enthusiastic. When viewed together, the images offered a journey into the past – a past which I remembered.

I asked for permission to mount the pictures on the Reading Libraries website and that permission was generously given.

My next task was to write a description of each image, using key words, to form the catalogue entry. In doing so I learned a lot about this part of town and thought that the pictures might form the basis of an exhibition. Then it occurred to me that the exhibition might form part of a local history study day – a series of talks and a walk round the area which is close to the library.

The exhibition and study day took place in 2009. They were greatly enjoyed and several people suggested that the photographs should be used as the basis for a book.

Now that the book has come about, we have a more permanent record of this area of mid-nineteenth-century Reading which has now changed beyond recognition.

In the Middle Ages the land had belonged to Reading Abbey. After the fall of the Abbey it remained in the hands of the Crown until the 1830s, when it was decided to sell off the land which bordered the Kennet Navigation, then at the peak of its importance. Since there were no roads nearby, King's Road and its bridges were built and the land between the new road and the Kennet was divided into lots and sold.

The great and expanding biscuit firm of Huntley & Palmers, which moved to a site on King's Road in 1846, did not play a direct role in buying up land and building houses for their employees as has been supposed. Many developers were involved in the 1840s and 1850s.

Some of these streets were named after Queen Victoria and her family, reflecting the time when the houses were built. She married Prince Albert in 1840 and their sons, Princes Arthur and Leopold, were born in 1850 and 1853 respectively. Rupert Street was probably named after Prince Rupert who fought on the Royalist side in the Civil War. The name of Orts Road is much older; the 'orts' were the scraps of food handed out to the poor people on behalf of the monks of Reading Abbey, which probably took place near Orts Bridge – on the site of the present-day Blake's Bridge on Forbury Road. Orts Farm included the land on which part of Newtown was built.

It is this first phase of the development which is pictured in this book – buildings constructed before building regulations existed, which by the 1970s were considered unfit for human habitation. The local council issued compulsory purchase orders and appointed Broadway & Malyan as planners and architects for the replacement houses. Terry was commissioned by Broadway & Malyan to photograph the old buildings before they came down.

So we owe a debt of gratitude to Broadway & Malyan for their far-sightedness, and to Terry with his photographic skills and his artist's eye for the typical, the unusual and the atmospheric. The photographs are more than a dry documentary record – we can even see some of the local residents, unselfconsciously doing what they usually did.

I hope that all who buy or borrow this book will enjoy the pictures as much as I have done.

David Cliffe

CONTENTS

INTRODUCTION

The purpose of this book is to show the area known as Newtown in Reading before the redevelopment which took place in the mid to late 1970s. I will not try to give a full history of the area, which is well documented in several well-presented and informative books on this subject. I will instead give a description by way of photographs of the houses, the people, the environment and also the decay which had taken place by 1974. Mostly, I wanted to record the still vibrant and close knit society which prevailed in this unique part of Reading. Having said this book will not be an historical record of the area, I feel it is important to record how and why the photographs came to be taken. Newtown was identified by Reading Borough Council for redevelopment in 1970. Broadway & Malyan was an architectural practice based in Weybridge that opened its first satellite office on the first floor of St. John's Ambulance Brigade HQ in London Road, Reading. In 1974 the practice was fortunate to win the commission to redevelop the Newtown site. The two young, enthusiastic partners in charge of the Reading Office,

knowing the interest I had in photography (and maybe to get me out from under their feet!) gave me the job of recording the buildings in all the streets which were to be demolished. This was a job from heaven and not to be turned down. It was agreed I could set up a dark room in the basement of the office to produce the photographs.

The Newtown site covered some 16.5 acres (approx. 6.5 hectares). The area was bounded by Orts Road to the south, King's Road to the west, Kennet Side to the north and Rupert Street to the east. Within this site were a number of public houses, only four of which were considered to be worth retaining.

These were:

The Dove, Leopold Road
The Plasterers Arms, Rupert Street
The Jolly Anglers, Kennet Side
The Fisherman's Cottage, Kennet Side
(formerly The Fisherman's Rest)

The rest to be demolished were:

The Thames Tavern, Kennet Side
(formerly The Anglers Rest)

The Anglers Arms, Albert Road

The Leopold Arms, Leopold Road (already
converted to business premises)

The Rupert Arms, Rupert Street

The Carpenters Arms, Orts Road

The True Patriot, Orts Road (already
closed)

There were, therefore, ten public houses in a
relatively small area, but these were the only
licensed premises in the whole area known as
Newtown. The possible reasons for this are well
documented in other historical publications,
but briefly it appears that the land outside the
area to be redeveloped was originally Crown
Land, now in the ownership of the Goldsmid
family, who were Jewish, and James Wheble,
Roman Catholic. Whether their religion was the
reason for the lack of public houses is not known.
However, the commonly held belief that Quakers
owned the land appears to be untrue.

So I set about wandering around the streets
of Newtown recording everything that was
required by the brief. Fortunately this was when
photographers were able to take images of
people going about their everyday lives and of
children playing in their natural surroundings. On
more than one occasion I was asked, although
not seriously, if I was David Bailey! What
innocence we have now lost!

It was obvious that in some areas the houses
were in a very poor state of repair, even just
from external observation; what the interiors
were like I cannot say as the brief was just to
record the exteriors. Many others were still
habitable and seemed to be well maintained.
One overwhelming impression I had was of the
attention to detail the Victorian builders had
displayed in their work. The intricate brickwork
of the façades can clearly be seen from the
photographs. It should also be noted that the
streets were not set out in straight lines but
curved and diverged so you couldn't see what
lay ahead around the next corner. Internal

courtyards enclosed almost secret places only accessible to the local people. It seemed that this area was suffering the deprivation, and in some areas the desolation, brought about by what would now be considered a lack of understanding on the part of local government of the special qualities and characteristics of the buildings and residents of Newtown.

There was a fierce sense of belonging, of being an intrinsic part of this area, which made the residents take pride in living in Newtown. To demonstrate this, it was recorded in 1974 that 147 families, totalling 393 persons (of whom 166 were children), had expressed a desire to return to the development when completed. It did seem to me that this sense of belonging was very strong, yet it did not appear to encompass the area beyond and to the east of Rupert Street.

One item of minor importance – and yet hopefully of interest to the reader – was the decision taken by the partners of the practice to organize a pub crawl, for want of a better description, in order to visit each of the public houses that were destined to be demolished. It must be emphasized that this was necessary from an historical architectural perspective and was before the introduction of breathalyzers. We did however limit ourselves to a half pint in each hostelry. There was one establishment, which shall be nameless, which obviously did not expect so many punters, as the only lights on were the ones behind the counter. However, the landlady did eventually appear (maybe she was watching Coronation Street) and managed to find enough glasses to quench the thirst of her newly acquired customers.

I managed to obtain permission from Southern Gas to climb to the top of one of the gasometers in order to take aerial views of the development area. I had to give an undertaking that should I fall, Southern Gas would not be responsible for any damage I caused. Can anyone reading this believe what would happen in today's society where Health and Safety requirements reign supreme? Would I now have to take a lengthy course on how to climb an external staircase before being considered trained and intelligent enough not to try the current craze of tombstoning into the Kennet? Thankfully, I was able to take some photographs from this vantage point and they are included in this book. I obviously survived this experience, as did the gasometers, which were also left intact thanks in no small part to common sense which prevailed in that era.

Although the area had been run down and lots of buildings were vacant and boarded up, these photos show the intimate qualities of the Newtown development. Corner and mid-terrace shops, some derelict, others with customers about to enter, are revealed by close inspection of the photographs. There also seemed to be a special relationship with the River Kennet (for a short distance the Kennet and Avon Canal which passes through Blake's Lock). The walk alongside the river (or canal) was vibrant and yet quite peaceful. People were just looking, some fishing or simply enjoying the tranquil environment of this special place.

The intense pride of the residents of the area earmarked for redevelopment, even though there were parts which were very run down, seemed to me to end at the boundary with Cumberland Road to the east. Whether this was a fact I cannot be certain, but a strong feeling persisted with me all the time I spent taking this pictorial record.

All this raises the question of whether mass demolition would now be considered inappropriate and refurbishment of the houses now take precedence. I do realise there will always be a body of opinion that wants progress to prevail; that is their prerogative. In order to try to be fair and give the argument for this case, the last section of this book will cover phase 1 of the development completed in about 1980, including images of the new housing. There are also images of the residents and of children playing as they always used to.

In conclusion, I would like to record why this book has been published. I retired from the practice in 2005, but being the photographer I retained all the negatives taken of the redevelopment.

Sometime in 2008, having nothing better to do, I attempted to re-organise my photographic collection and came across the folder with the negatives and contact sheets. On a whim, I decided to contact Reading Central Library and was put in touch with David Cliffe, Local History Librarian. The rest is history, as recounted in David's Foreword.

Whilst the photographs may not be perfect and some have been affected by light entering the cassette, I do hope anyone reading this book will enjoy them as much as I did taking them.

1 OS MAPS & AERIAL VIEWS

The area covered by this book was offered for sale in 1833 by the Crown which had appropriated it from Reading Abbey upon its dissolution in 1539. Most of the site was bought by one-time mayor Thomas Lawrence and built up very slowly at first: maps drawn in 1834 and 1840 show only two buildings, almost certainly the pairs of semi-detatched houses at 184–186 and 196–198 Kennet Side, already demolished by the time these photos were taken. Most of the other houses went up between 1855 and 1864; they were spacious by the standards of the time, and many groups and terraces had individual names.

The maps are from the 1957 Ordnance Survey edition. The aerial views are taken from the top of a gasometer belonging to Southern Gas. For these photographs to be taken I had to get written permission from Southern Gas, who were very cooperative and understanding of what I needed to achieve. The four views show the entire area of the proposed development. On the individual photographs I have tried to identify buildings which may be of particular interest.

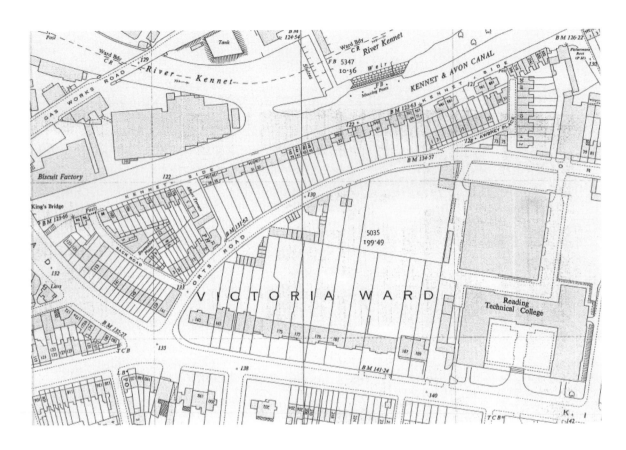

Map 1: The area from King's Road proceeding
eastwards. The streets primarily featured in
the photographs are: Awbrey Place/Terrace,
Kennet Side (part) and Orts Road (part).

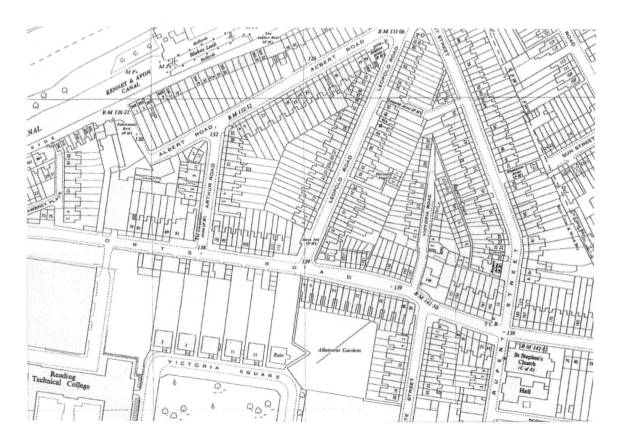

Map 2: A continuation of Map 1 proceeding
east. The streets primarily featured in the
photographs are: Leopold Road, Rupert Street,
Victoria Road, Kingsgate Street, Orts Road (part)
and Sun Street.

Map 3: A continuation of Map 2 proceeding
north. The streets primarily featured in the
photographs are: Albert Road (part),
Kennet Side (part), Leopold Road (part),
Orts Road (part) and Rupert Street (part).
The large circles in the top right-hand
corner are the gasometers from which the
photographs were taken.

View from the top of the gasometer with the
junction of Rupert Street and Leopold Road
in the centre foreground. A post office shop
is on the corner, with The Anglers Arms public
house on the right.

View from the top of the gasometer with Kennet Side in the foreground. The junction of Leopold Road and Albert Road is shown with The Anglers Arms public house on the corner. The end of Rupert Street is in the bottom left corner, with steps down to Kennet Side.

View from the top of the gasometer with
Kennet Side in the foreground. The white-
painted building is The Thames Tavern with
Blake's Lock beyond. Reading Technical College
is the large building in the background.

View from the top of the gasometer with New Town Junior School dominating the foreground. The area in the background was not affected by the redevelopment.

2   KENNET SIDE

This section covers the entire length of Kennet Side from King's Road through to and beyond the railway bridge. It features three public houses namely The Fisherman's Cottage (formerly The Fisherman's Rest), The Thames Tavern (formerly The Anglers Rest) and The Jolly Anglers. Other points of interest are Blake's Lock, New Town Junior School and the railway bridge over the River Kennet. A number of properties fronting Kennet Side are shown on the 1957 OS map with two sets of house numbers, suggesting that they were double houses or 'back-to-backs' with windows facing only one way. But street directories list them only under Orts Road or Albert Road, so it seems they were in fact single houses with two entrances and at some stage they changed their addresses because access for cars and deliveries was easier from the 'back' side than from the narrow towpath.

In order to take the photographs I needed to gain access to the island between the Kennet and Avon Canal and the River Kennet. The photographs show that Kennet Side was well used by pedestrians, people are fishing in the river and generally enjoying the peaceful environment. Cruisers are also shown on the waterway.

For the location of this section, refer to Maps 1 & 3.

The bottom of steps down from King's Road on the right. The True Patriot public house (already closed) is in the background on the right. Back Road and Devonshire Place houses have already been demolished.

The house nearest the camera is No.126
Kennet Side, with a separate entrance from
No.23 Orts Road. A painted sign 'Awbrey
Cottages' can be seen on the end wall.
Girls are pushing prams and walking a dog
alongside the River Kennet.

Taken from the island looking towards
King's Road. Children are looking at the
River Kennet. The Borough Arms can be
seen in the centre background. The houses
in Kennet Side have separate entraces to
Orts Road.

Taken from the island looking downstream on
the River Kennet. The substantial houses on
the left are Nos.174 to 168, then 166 to 156
Kennet Side. These have separate entrances
in Orts Road.

Taken from the island looking towards
King's Road in the far distance. The houses
from left to right are Nos.160 to 126, with 154
to 142 being three-storey. Nos.134 & 136 are
painted white. The posts in the foreground
are in front of the weir. I chose this photo for
the front cover as I think it embodies all that
the book is about.

Taken from the island looking upstream from
Blake's Lock. The Fisherman's Cottage public
house is just beyond the four-storey houses
Nos.226–228. Nos.222–184 have already been
demolished, showing Awbrey Terrace beyond.

Taken from the island looking downstream
at Blake's Lock. The white-painted Thames
Tavern (previously called The Anglers Rest)
is opposite the lock. The houses beyond are
Nos.268–312 Kennet Side.

A photograph of Blake's Lock on the Kennet
and Avon Canal with the cruiser 'Sun Dial'
moored up. The three and four-storey
Nos.262–226 lead up to The Fisherman's
Cottage, just visible round the corner beyond
the lock-keeper.

More general view of Blake's Lock taken from the island with the edge of the white-painted Thames Tavern just visible on the left-hand side with the three-storey terrace of houses leading up towards The Fisherman's Cottage public house, not in view.

Taken from the island with The Jolly Anglers
public house on the right and two men
fishing. The two houses on the left of the pub
are Nos.318 and 320, with Nos.322 to 334
demolished for the sitting area. New Town
Junior school is just visible in the background.

Taken from the island looking upstream with
the sitting area on the left-hand side. Two
remaining houses lead up to The Jolly Anglers
public house with two men fishing in the
Kennet. Then the terrace of houses leads up
to the white-painted Thames Tavern in the far
distance.

Two girls in mini-skirts in the sitting area where Nos.322–334 have been demolished and children playing on the grassed bank at the back. A boy with a fishing rod walks by on the right.

A more general view taken from the island with the sitting area towards the right-hand end. There are children playing in front of the sitting area and a lady with a pushchair in front of the terrace of houses Nos.336–346.

Looking upstream from the island with posts protecting the weir in the centre foreground. The houses starting from the left are Nos.154–142 (three-storey), Nos.140–126 with Nos.136 and 134 painted white.

A view from the island with the entrance to
The Fisherman's Cottage public house on the
extreme left-hand side. A terrace of houses
Nos.222–208 is in the centre foreground
with a gap where Nos.198–194 have been
demolished. The deck of a barge moored to
the island is in the foreground.

Taken from the Southern Gas site with boys
fishing near the steps leading down from
Rupert Street to Kennet Side. The gable of
the house on the left belongs to No.116
Rupert Street. The white-painted building
in the distance is The Thames Tavern.

A view from the island with a girl pushing a pram in front of the gap where Nos.222–184 have been demolished. The three-storey houses in the distance commence at No.174.

A view from the Southern Gas site with
washing on lines behind houses in Albert
Road. Steps leading down from Rupert Street
to Kennet Side are immediately in front of the
white-painted house, No.116 Rupert Street.

The steps leading down from Rupert Street
to Kennet Side. The building immediately
beyond is the Post Office on the corner of
Leopold Road and Rupert Street. The shop with
a boarded up window is No.85 Albert Road.

A view from the Southern Gas site showing
the terrace of houses Nos.346–336 leading
up to New Town Junior School which can be
seen on the far left. The gasometer is behind
the trees.

Men and boys fishing in the River Kennet
beyond the railway bridge. A cruiser is shown
passing underneath the bridge. New Town
Junior School can be seen just beneath the
brick arch on the left.

A view from Kennet Side under the brick arched railway bridge with New Town Junior School in the immediate foreground.

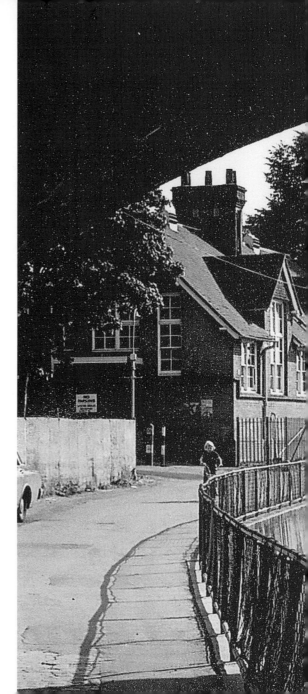

3 ALBERT ROAD

This section is devoted to Albert Road. This runs in a north-easterly direction from The Fisherman's Cottage public house at the west end to Rupert Street at the east end. Arthur Road and Leopold Road join it at two points. At the junction with Leopold Road stands The Anglers Arms public house with an interesting brick porch facing Albert Road. Another building to note is the double-fronted residence No.32/34 which has an arched access to No.32A, formerly St. John's Mission Room. The houses on the north side (odd Nos.) are all built with separate entrances to Kennet Side.

For the location of this section, refer to Maps 2 & 3.

A group of children, maybe a family, playing with cardboard boxes in the front garden of No.25 which has a separate entrance to No.252 Kennet Side.

No.32/34 with an archway through to No.32A,
the former St. John's Mission Room. Note
the semi-circular arch over the second floor
window with a stone plaque below denoting
'Berry Place'.

A close-up of the archway in No.32/34 with the entrance to No.32A, the former St. John's Mission Room.

A view through the archway in No.32/34 with the now derelict and boarded up houses Nos.49 and 51 Albert Road which have separate entrances to Nos.276 and 278 Kennet Side.

A view through the wrought iron garden gate looking at No.9 Albert Road, with what appear to be cabbages growing in the garden. To the left is No.7. These have separate entrances to Nos.232 and 234 Kennet Side.

The three-storey houses are Nos.69 and 71 with an abandoned Mini parked in front of No.71. The two-storey house on the left is No.67 Albert Road. These have separate entrances to Nos.308 to 312 Kennet Side.

The back of The Thames Tavern (formerly The Anglers Rest). The terraced houses to the left are Nos.31–37 with the white-painted ones being Nos.25–29. The houses beyond with dormer windows are Nos.21 and 23. The whole row have separate entrances to Nos.248–264 Kennet Side.

The house on the extreme right of the photograph is No.21 with the remaining terrace of both two and three-storey properties being Nos.1–19 Albert Road. These have separate entrances to Nos.226–246 Kennet Side.

The terrace of two-storey houses are
Nos.51–67, with the three-storey dwellings
with feature gables being Nos.69 and 71.
These have separate entrances to
Nos.278–310 Kennet Side.

This is a more general view of the properties
on Albert Road. The dwellings with dormers
in the central foreground are Nos.21 and 23.
These have separate entrances to Kennet Side.

The passageway at the side of the
derelict house, No.1 Albert Road. In the
left foreground are the outbuildings of
The Fisherman's Cottage public house.
Children can just be seen walking up the
passageway towards the photographer.
The stone-built section of the wall could
be of medieval origin.

A derelict and boarded up corner shop, No.85 Albert Road. Rupert Street is on the right where steps lead down to Kennet Side. The two and three-storey houses to the left are Nos.71–83.

A group of girls in front of The Anglers Arms.
They are reacting in a most happy and natural
way to having their photograph taken.

The same group of girls in front of The Anglers Arms public house. The three-storey house just above the heads of the girls is No.32/34 and the entrance to the former St. John's Mission Room.

The start of Albert Road with part of
No.1 just visible. The road in poor state of
repair leads down to Kennet Side with
The Fisherman's Cottage public house on
the left. The pub sign can also be seen and,
possibly, the Blake's Lock lock-keeper in the
far distance.

Taken from Orts Road with Nos.1–19 seen before the partly demolished wall which hides Nos.21–23. Nos.73–75 Orts Road and Nos.2–20 Awbrey Terrace have already been demolished.

4 AWBREY PLACE & ARTHUR ROAD

This section covers the two streets at the back of, and on either side of The Fisherman's Cottage public house on Kennet Side, Awbrey Place (or Terrace) and Arthur Road. Both are accessed from Orts Road and are quite short but no less interesting for that. For instance on a generally level and flat site, Awbrey Terrace had a distinct incline down towards Kennet Side as one of the photographs will show. The even Nos. in Awbrey Place had already been demolished, whereas Arthur Road remained pretty well intact. The Carpenters Arms public house was situated at the corner of Arthur Road and Orts Road and is included in this section of photographs. At the end of Awbrey Place at the junction with Kennet Side a play area had been constructed, presumably by the local children (with, it must be said, help from older residents). This had been done using any bits of material they could find, including a large diameter concrete pipe. It was somewhere the children could play in a place made by and for them. Fortunately Health and Safety zealots do not seem to have been aware of the dangers a structure such as this could present!

For the location of this section, refer to Map 1.

No.1 Awbrey Terrace on the extreme right-hand side with a girl pushing an old-fashioned pram, the wheels of which were much sought after by children. The houses in the background are in Orts Road and have separate entrances to Kennet Side.

A view from Orts Road of Awbrey Terrace with
Nos.9–13 running from left to right. Behind the
tree, Nos.2–20 have already been demolished,
enabling us to see part of the smoke-house of
John Eighteen the fishmonger. The gasometer
is visible in the far distance.

This is taken from the bottom of the road, with some of the odd-numbered houses on the right. Chestnut paling fences have been erected in front of the empty dwellings and there are posts across the road.

An interesting photograph taken from Orts Road showing on the left No.23. To the right is the play area created by the local residents where Nos.2–20 Awbrey Terrace and Nos.208–222 Kennet Side have been demolished. The white-painted building behind the play area is The Fisherman's Cottage public house.

A close-up view of the play area created by
the residents, and no doubt the children, to
provide an area for them to enjoy, in what
was a simpler and more adventurous era. The
painted homage to a well-known football
team can be seen on the main structural post.

At the junction of Arthur Road and Orts Road
The Carpenters Arms can just be seen on the
left-hand side, with the rear of No.95 Orts
Road on the right. The terrace of two and
three-storey houses on the right are Nos.2–20.

At the junction of Arthur Road and
Orts Road the rear of The Carpenters Arms
can be seen on the left-hand side. The terrace
of two-storey houses on the left is Nos.3–11.
Albert Road is in the distance with the flues of
Southern Gas rising up behind.

Taken from the corner of Arthur Road and
Albert Road. The two and three-storey houses
are from No.14 where two ladies are walking
by, to No.2 in the distance. Some of the
façades of the houses have been modernised
with pebble-dash, or rendered and painted.

5 ORTS ROAD

The photographs in this section were all taken in Orts Road, which runs in a west to east direction starting at King's Road through to and beyond Rupert Street which was the limit of the redevelopment area. Demolition had already commenced at the western end; Back Lane, Devonshire Place, Albert Terrace being the affected streets. The True Patriot public house was still standing but had already closed. The Carpenter's Arms and The Dove were public houses which at the time still remained open for trading. However, The Carpenter's Arms was due to be demolished. The smoke-houses belonging to John Eighteen, the fishermonger, are shown to be still standing but, as far as is known, were not in use.

For the location of this section, refer to Maps 1 & 2.

The houses shown are Nos.59–71, the last
four being quite substantial properties and,
judging by the washing on the lines are
still occupied. These houses have separate
entrances to Nos.162–174 Kennet Side. The
gasometer can clearly be seen in the distance.

The arched entrance to what was John
Eighteen, the fishmonger's smoke-houses.
It's now derelict but had previously been
converted and used as a garage business. The
terraced houses to the right are Nos.79–83.
All are now vacant.

The north side of Orts Road; Nos.125–131,
then a passageway, continuing with
Nos.133–147 to the corner of Victoria Road.
Children are playing on the pavement outside
No.127. Above this house is a plaque reading
'Victoria Terrace'.

A more detailed photograph of a row of five terraced houses, Nos.123–135 Orts Road, showing the plaque reading 'Victoria Terrace' over No.127. This photograph shows the brick detailing between ground-floor and first-floor windows.

VICTORIA ROAD
NO THROUGH ROAD

149

A fine example of a detached Victorian villa, No.149, named 'La Chateau' (sic). Victoria Road is to the left of this house with Nos.147–143 on the left of Victoria Road.

A public telephone box in use with a Chopper
bicycle leant against the pavement. This is on
the corner of Rupert Street and Orts Road with
Nos.163–151 to the left. The porch of No.149
can just be seen at the extreme left-hand side.

Orts Road looking towards St. Stephen's
Church in the distance, taken from the corner
of Victoria Road, with a boarded up shop on
the corner of Kingsgate Street and Orts Road.
The houses beyond the shop are Nos.44–54
Orts Road.

Looking east along the north side of Orts
Road with Nos.165–197. These are opposite
St. Stephen's Church and the eastern
boundary of the redevelopment area.

The junction of Orts Road and Victoria Road
with Nos.147–121 on the right-hand side.
The Dove public house can be seen in the
distance.

A public telephone box sited on the corner of Rupert Street and Orts Road, looking down towards Kingsgate Street with a corner shop, No.40 Orts Road, in the middle distance. The houses on left are Nos.54–46, those on the right Nos.163–151.

A view along Orts Road looking west towards
Rupert Street with St. Stephen's Church on the
left-hand side. The houses to the left, Nos.60–56
and Nos.197–165 to the right, formed the
eastern boundary of the redevelopment area.
The shop in the far distance is No.40 Orts Road.

The bay window of No.195
Orts Road with an old gas lantern
over the window. It is possible this was
a former off licence. It seems to be the
only property that had a basement.

A group of children playing on the pavement
outside properties in Orts Road, possibly
Nos.99 and 101.

Two children leaning on the garden wall and posing for the photographer. The property is possibly No.99 or 101 Orts Road.

The yard and dilapidated outbuildings at the rear of the smoke-houses of John Eighteen, fishmonger, now being used as a dumping ground.

6 RUPERT STREET, KINGSGATE STREET & SUN STREET

This section covers three streets at the eastern extremity of the redevelopment area; Rupert Street, Kingsgate Street and Sun Street. A few of the houses were already vacant and boarded up but most were still occupied. Two public houses, The Plasterers Arms and The Rupert Arms, were, at the time the photographs were taken, still trading. The latter was demolished in the redevelopment. Both fronted onto Rupert Street. The Plasterers Arms is reputed to have been the regular haunt of the TV personality Melvyn Bragg (now Lord Bragg of Wigton). This however, has not been verified. At the northern end of Rupert Street there is an incline with, at the bottom, steps down to Kennet Side.

For the location of this section, refer to Maps 2 & 3.

Looking south along Rupert Street with
The Plasterers Arms just beyond the two
three-storey buildings. The houses on the
left running towards The Plasterers Arms are
Nos.64–42.

Rupert Street looking north with No.43 in the near foreground and the boarded up Little's Stores and the nameplate 'Rupert Court' above the alleyway. A girl is walking by on the right-hand side with a child running across the road, possibly going to Rupert Court.

A close-up view of No.43, boarded up
with the alleyway to Rupert Court next door.
Little's Stores is boarded up with graffiti
recording a well known 1970s pop group.

RUPERT COURT

LITTLE'S S

SLADE

Looking south along Rupert Street at the
bend in the road, with the Rupert Arms and
Nos.21–27 to the right. Nos.23 and 25 have
apparently been converted to commercial/
retail use.

Rupert Street looking north, taken from
outside The Rupert Arms looking towards
The Plasterers Arms in the middle distance.
The gasometer is clearly visible in the
background.

A detailed view of the two houses,
Nos.36 and 34, adjoining The Plasterers Arms,
showing feature bands of brickwork which
have been painted white on No.34.

The terraced houses at the northern end
of Rupert Street, Nos.102–116. No.100 has
already been demolished. On the extreme
left-hand side, steps lead down to Kennet
Side. The gasometer is a dominant feature
behind the houses.

A view of the backs of Nos. 102–116 Rupert Street. No.100 has already been demolished. No.102, including its outbuilding, is in a poor state of repair and is obviously boarded up and vacant.

Looking north along Kingsgate Street with Nos.2–20 on the left and Nos.3–25 on the right. The house in the distance is No.149 Orts Road.

A view taken further down Kingsgate Street showing a Clifford's milk float making a delivery and people talking outside No.12 Kingsgate Street. The house facing Kingsgate Street is No.149 Orts Road, called 'La Chateau' (sic).

Taken in Sun Street looking towards the back of The Plasterers Arms public house in Rupert Street.

7 LEOPOLD ROAD & VICTORIA ROAD

The photographs in this section are taken in Leopold Road and Victoria Road, both are accessed from Orts Road and run in a generally northern direction. Leopold Road links up with Albert Road but Victoria Road, much shorter in length, is a cul-de-sac. Leopold Road orginally had three public houses: The Anglers Arms at the junction with Albert Road, The Dove which fronted onto Orts Road and The Leopold Arms which had closed to become a plant hire shop. There is a corner shop, which was still trading when the photographs were taken, on the corner of Orts Road opposite The Dove public house. At the other end of Leopold Road, on the corner of Rupert Street, was the local Post Office.

For the location of this section, refer to Maps 2 & 3.

The shop premises facing Orts Road with the start of Leopold Road on the left. The house with the ornate canopy over the entrance is No.2, with just part of a double-fronted house, No.4, to the left.

This shows the ornate canopy to No.2 with the double-fronted, more substantial house to the left being No.4. The houses running on from this are Nos.6–26 with the alleyway providing access to Florence Place. The nameplate is just visible on the black-painted three-storey house which can be seen behind the two children running along the pavement.

This section of terraced houses on the eastern side of the street runs from No.32 up to No.50. The former public house, The Leopold Arms, has now closed to become a hire shop. The houses in the far distance are in Rupert Street.

Catchpoles

Hithcock .

Wyatts .

This section of terraced houses on the western side of the street runs from No.25 down to The Anglers Arms on the corner of Albert Road. The three-storey house with a gabled front is No.43. The houses just visible behind the gentleman in the black coat are in Rupert Street.

The rear and side of The Anglers Arms at the junction with Albert Road. The young boy in flared trousers is standing outside the back gate to No.46 Albert Road.

A general view taken from the junction with
Albert Road looking south. The Anglers Arms
is just visible on the right, with two young boys
playing on the pavement on the left. The plant
hire shop, formerly The Leopold Arms, can
also be seen on the left.

This shows a group of young people, maybe
from the same family, in the front garden of
No.48. The young boy on the extreme left
also appears in the preceding photograph.
Obviously he was not camera shy!

Two young girls standing on the pavement in Leopold Road quite unconcerned and happy to pose for the photographer. The age of innocence is now sadly lost.

Victoria Road. This first view is taken from one
end of the terrace of houses on the right-hand
side starting with No.2. The houses on the left
are Nos.3–37. The distinctive property, No.7,
behind the 'mini-van', is slightly wider than
most and seems to have been a shop with a
projecting fascia over the window.

A more detailed photograph looking
particularly at the distinctive property, No.7,
which seems to show more clearly that
this was a shop. It had a projecting fascia
with moulded corbels at each end over the
window, which has been modified to make it
more suited to domestic use.

This photograph is taken from the lower end
and shows the kerbs ending outside No.27,
although the road continues in order to give
access to the rest of the properties. A section
of the pavement has a balustrade erected,
presumably because the drop from pavement
to road has increased.

This photograph is taken at a low level from
the end of Victoria Road to try to show the
incline up towards Orts Road. The terrace
of houses in heavy shade on the left are
Nos.2–14. The property partly hidden behind
the Clifford's Dairies milk float is No.40, the
shop in Orts Road.

8   PUBLIC HOUSES

The Newtown site to be redeveloped, although only 16.5 acres, boasted a wealth of public houses. There were originally ten within the site. When the photographs were taken in 1974 only eight were still trading. Two had closed: The True Patriot in Orts Road, quite close to Back Lane, and The Leopold Arms, in Leopold Road, which had been converted into a plant hire shop. Kennet Side boasted three: The Fisherman's Cottage (formerly The Fisherman's Rest), The Thames Tavern (formerly The Anglers Rest) and The Jolly Anglers.

Orts Road could be said to have two remaining, although each was on a corner with another street: The Carpenters Arms (Arthur Road) and The Dove (Leopold Road). The ones in Rupert Street were not on corner sites and these were The Rupert Arms and the Plasterers Arms. The last one was The Anglers Arms which again was on a corner between Albert Road and Leopold Road. So it could be said that Leopold Road once had three licensed premises along its fairly short length. Quite a record some might contend! It should be noted that not all the pubs have been included in this section as others are featured in the various streets recorded elsewhere.

For the location of this section, refer to Maps 1, 2 & 3.

The Thames Tavern. The name was changed
from The Anglers Rest, possibly to save confusion
with The Jolly Anglers and The Fisherman's Rest
(now The Fisherman's Cottage), both on Kennet
Side. The photograph was taken from the island
adjoining Blake's Lock and shows in the foreground,
the paddle wheel which operates the lock.

A photograph of The Jolly Anglers which is the last one down-stream on Kennet Side. It was taken from the Southern Gas property on the other side of the River Kennet. Maybe it is no coincidence that a man and boy are fishing in the river!

A view of The Carpenters Arms in Orts Road. The photograph was taken to show the side elevation facing Arthur Road. Two children on a Chopper bicycle are riding along the pavement. A man is working on the front elevation of No.91 Orts Road.

VERY

HENLEY · THE DO

PUBLIC BAR

LEOPOLD ROAD

Another view of The Dove in Orts Road at the corner of Leopold Road. This photograph was taken to show the side elevation of the building.

The final view of The Dove in Orts Road on
the corner of Leopold Road. This photograph
was taken to show the front elevation of the
building and the relationship to the local shop
on the corner of Leopold Road. Children can
be seen going into the shop.

The Rupert Arms in Rupert Street. It was close
to, but not on the junction with Orts Road.
The lady in front of the pub may have been
the landlady.

The first of two photographs taken showing
The Plasterers Arms in Rupert Street. This view
from the left-hand side shows a Ferguson's
Wine Merchant van parked outside. Could this
have been making a delivery?

A second photograph taken showing
The Plasterers Arms in Rupert Street. This
view from the right-hand side shows the
relationship with the adjoining houses, with
the gasometer rising up behind the three-
storey houses on the left.

I make no apology for completing this section with three photographs of The Anglers Arms on the corner of Leopold Road and Arthur Road. This one is a front view showing the position of the pub with Leopold Road on the left and Arthur Road on the right. There can still be seen to the right of the window at first-floor level a painted sign reading FULLY LICENSED.

A detail of the brick-built porch entrance to The Anglers Arms fronting Albert Road. The Courage Group sign is obvious beyond the porch.

The final photograph of this section, if not my favourite, must come very close. It again shows The Anglers Arms, but this time with a group of children standing and posing for my benefit in front of the public house. If only a photograph like this could be taken now!

9 COMPLETED DEVELOPMENT

In about 1980, of my own volition, I decided to revisit the now partially completed development. The first phase of the four was centred on the houses fronting the River Kennet starting from King's Road and proceeding eastwards. Where possible the original names of the streets or culs-de-sac were reused. Naturally Kennet Side remained and Orts Road was still the main thoroughfare, although now not a through route. Further east, Canal Way, Lock Place and Avon Place were used to reflect the proximity of the river.

I have not, in this section, identified individual houses but just named the streets or culs-de-sacs. I have again, tried to photograph ordinary people going about their everyday lives and children playing in the newly developed environment. I leave it to readers to judge for themselves whether the redevelopment is and was a success.

This photograph, taken from the Huntley &
Palmers site, shows two cyclists riding along
Kennet Side at the junction with Patriot Place
and the roadway, as yet unmade. The three-
storey flats with Juliet balconies enjoy views
along the River Kennet.

Taken from Orts Road, showing the houses in
Patriot Place. Children can be seen playing in
and just outside the front gardens. Two ladies
are talking while the children play. The three-
storey flats on the extreme left are the ones
facing Kennet Side.

The first of three photographs taken in Albert
Place. It is a view looking westwards.
The houses and back gardens of the dwellings
on the right are those facing Kennet Side.

The second of three photographs taken
in Albert Place. It is a view looking at the
dwellings in the north west corner.
The stepped access down to Kennet Side is
clearly seen to the right of the man looking
out from the rear entrance of his house.

The last of three photographs of Albert Place
seen from Orts Road with two ladies passing
by. The stepped access to Kennet Side can
just be seen on the extreme left.

The first of two photographs taken in Avon Place. It is looking at the houses fronting Kennet Side with a man standing at the entrance to the stepped access down to the canal. The houses to the left do not seem to be occupied.

The second of two photographs taken in Avon Place, looking in the opposite direction. A dog seems to be interested in what I am doing, while the man in a peaked hat seems to find it amusing. An arched access can be seen above the car parked on the left.

This photograph shows Rupert Place with
four people approaching The Plasterers
Arms. It may be that the Mock Tudor façade
is somewhat incongruous set against the new
development. On a later visit I was shocked
to find that The Plasterers Arms has now been
demolished to make way for a block of flats!

Taken from the Southern Gas site. The
substantial posts and rail are to protect the
sluices on the River Kennet which is in the
foreground. The Kennet and Avon Canal
can just be seen in the distance.

New Town Junior School is just out of sight on
the left. Several people can be seen walking
or riding along Kennet Side.

This is the final photograph. It is not located,
but is on the Newtown development.
I leave the reader to add a caption.

Two Rivers Press has been publishing in and about Reading since 1994. Founded by the artist Peter Hay (1951–2003), the press continues to delight readers, local and further afield, with its varied list of individually designed, thought-provoking books.